Super Spiders

Contents | **Page**

written by Pam Holden

Spiders live all over the world.

Some spiders live in
trees and gardens.

All spiders have eight legs.

They can jump and
climb and run fast.

Some spiders make webs to catch insects.

insect

The webs are sticky.

Some spiders have six eyes.

Some have eight eyes.

Some spiders are red or black or brown.

Some spiders are white or green or orange.

Some spiders are hairy like this one.

It is as big as your hand.

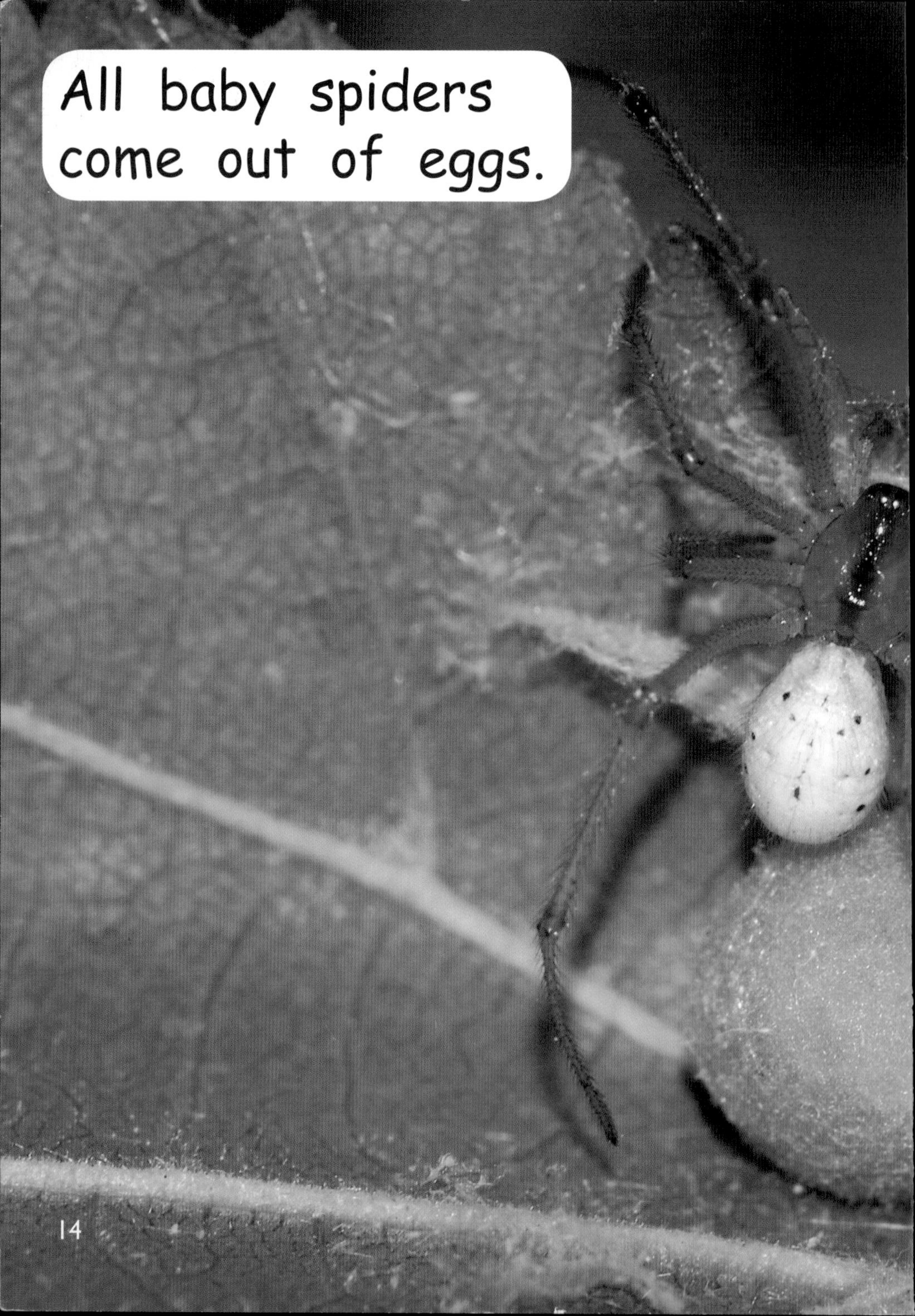

All baby spiders come out of eggs.

Some mother spiders make nests for the baby spiders.

nest

Birds like to eat spiders. The spiders have to hide from hungry birds!